Under the Greenwood Tree

In this series

I'M NOBODY! WHO ARE YOU?
Poems of Emily Dickinson for Young People
illustrated by Rex Schneider

A SWINGER OF BIRCHES
Poems of Robert Frost for Young People
illustrated by Peter Koeppen

William Shakespeare

Under the Greenwood Tree

Shakespeare for Young People

**Illustrated by
Robin and Pat DeWitt**

with an Introduction by A.L. Rowse

Edited by Barbara Holdridge

Stemmer
House
PUBLISHERS, INC.

Owings Mills, Maryland

Inquiries should be directed to
Stemmer House Publishers, Inc.
2627 Caves Road
Owings Mills, Maryland 21117

A Barbara Holdridge book
Printed and bound in Hong Kong
First Edition

Library of Congress Cataloging-in-Publication Data

Shakespeare, William, 1564-1616.
  Under the greenwood tree.

  "A Barbara Holdridge book"—Verso of t.p.
  Summary: An illustrated collection of poetic
excerpts from the plays and sonnets of Shakespeare,
following the "seven ages of man" pattern from
childhood fantasy to old age.
  1. Children's poetry, English. [1. English poetry]
I. DeWitt, Robin, ill. II. DeWitt, Pat, ill.
PR2771   1986   822.3'3   86-3686
ISBN 0-88045-028-2
ISBN 0-88045-029-0 (pbk.)

95-50

Contents

Introduction

THESE POEMS AND PICTURES are to be enjoyed together for their own sakes. They also give us a good idea of what William Shakespeare was like, the background of his life, his range of interests, and the sources of his inspiration.

He was born in 1564 at Stratford-upon-Avon, an old town beside the little river, in Warwickshire in the heart of England. His mother was Mary Arden, an heiress in a small way, of an old family of gentlefolk, who came from the Forest of Arden, the woodland country to the north of the town. The lovely song "Under the Greenwood Tree," comes from his play, *As You Like It*, which mostly takes place in the greenwood of the Forest of Arden.

That song gave the title to a beautiful novel by Thomas Hardy, *Under the Greenwood Tree*; for Shakespeare's work, plays and poems, have inspired more writers, artists, composers of music, than any other writer. Shakespeare, himself the foremost writer in our language whom we have given to the world, became the world's greatest playwright.

His father, John, was a glover who busied himself in the town's affairs, and became an alderman, a leading councillor. Notice that his son tells us that Queen Mab among the fairies is

> In shape no bigger than an agate stone
> On the forefinger of an alderman.

A favourite poem of mine is his winter poem, "When icicles hang by the wall." How it brings winter home to us, in a strangely cosy way—the winters of his own time, four hundred years ago, when the milk was brought into the little town in pails from the farm outside. And the logs of wood are carried in for a blazing fire on the wide-open hearth— just as we see it in his childhood's home at Stratford.

He was a countryman born, and always remained one at heart, retiring to his native country town after his busy, hard-working life away. We see this all through his work and in many of these extracts from it. He had a particular fondness for flowers, both garden and wild, his favourite being roses. But he noticed everything—every kind of bird, hedgehogs, snails, newts, beetles; he was specially conscious of snakes, though all except one, the adder, are harmless in England. As Thomas Hardy writes, 'He was one who used to notice such things.'

He loved country folklore and was inspired by it: Queen Mab and the fairies leaving their prints in the dew—fairy-rings we still called them in my youth; Puck or Robin Goodfellow playing his tricks; Ariel, serving the magician Prospero in the enchanted island; witches, like those in *Macbeth*. This country lore filled his imagination and is largely the stuff of which *A Midsummer Night's Dream* was made. Then there were the country craftsmen he observed, and made fun of lovingly: Bottom the weaver, Quince the carpenter, Snug a joiner, Flute who mended bellows (to blow up the fire), Snout the tinker. In other plays we have a whole array of such characters: country curates; pedlars and thieves; simple bumpkins; schoolmasters—William had been one for a time, before becoming an actor and taking to the roads.

His mind was tuned to the past, his imagination stirred by the great events and characters of the ancient world Julius Caesar, Brutus and Coriolanus; Cleopatra and Antony. But especially was he stirred by the exciting events of the previous century in England, the drama of the Wars of the Roses, a civil war between two branches of the royal family, with the feuds it let loose in the country. Also there was the long duel for mastery with France across the Channel.

Shakespeare was more a man of the theatre than any great writer has ever been. He began as an actor, but with a wife and three children to support before he was twenty-one, he had a long uphill struggle. He had, however, plenty of confidence to support him—and he was very anxious to do well and succeed. We know that he was a good actor, though not a star: that was his colleague Richard Burbage, to whom Shakespeare left money in his will for a ring to remember him by.

In earlier years he did a good deal of touring around the country, observing everything as usual: people's characters and oddities—"humours," as he called them; buildings, especially monuments in churches, and the abbey ruins from the recent Reformation, "bare ruined choirs, where late the sweet birds sang." Then he went on to writing plays, usually two a year, one comedy, one tragedy or history play.

He took his share in producing and all the business of his company, especially after the Lord Chamberlain's Company was founded in 1594, when Shakespeare was thirty. The Lord Chamberlain was a first cousin of Queen Elizabeth I—Shakespeare her favourite dramatist (and everybody else's). His generous young patron, the Earl of Southhampton, helped him to buy a share in the Company at its formation. Thenceforward he worked along with those fellows for the rest of his life, becoming the premier theatre company in London. Eventually, when they bought the Blackfriars theatre, Shakespeare became a part-owner of it.

Most plays took place in the open air in those days, and even the theatres were partly open to the skies, except for the galleries. But Shakespeare's Company were so successful that they were able to buy the Blackfriars theatre for indoor playing.

The year afterwards a ship, the *Sea Venture*, was voyaging out to Virginia when a terrific hurricane wrecked it on the coast of Bermuda. The ship broke up, but not a life was lost. The colonists spent the winter there, and in the spring built a small boat from the ship's timbers and sailed on to Jamestown, the first colony. A letter describing all this came back to Blackfriars, and Shakespeare made it the subject of his beautiful play, *The Tempest*, the next to the last that he wrote.

He was living, partly retired by then, at Stratford, in a big house he had bought just across the lane from the grammar school he had attended as a boy. (The recent headmaster there was my pupil.) Shakespeare's wife was ageing now—she was eight or nine years older. Daughter Susanna and her husband, with their child, looked after the household. They inherited the considerable property the father had built up by his lifetime of hard work, in and around his native town with the ancient bridge that took him away to fame and fortune. Yet all the family were gathered together before the altar, in that splendid church they had attended Sunday by Sunday. And we may use his own words for his epitaph:

> Fear no more the heat of the sun,
>   Nor the furious winter's rages;
> Thou thy worldly task hast done,
>   Home art gone, and ta'en thy wages.

A. L. Rowse

Cornwall, England
February 1986

Under the greenwood tree
Who loves to lie with me,
And turn his merry note
Unto the sweet bird's throat,
Come hither, come hither, come hither:
Here shall he see
No enemy
But winter and rough weather.

(*As You Like It*, Act II, scene vii)

9

When icicles hang by the wall,
    And Dick the shepherd blows his nail,
And Tom bears logs into the hall,
    And milk comes frozen home in pail,
When blood is nipp'd, and ways be foul,
Then nightly sings the staring owl,

Tu-whit;

Tu-who, a merry note,
While greasy Joan doth keel the pot.

When all aloud the wind doth blow,
    And coughing drowns the parson's saw,
And birds sit brooding in the snow,
    And Marian's nose looks red and raw,
When roasted crabs hiss in the bowl,
Then nightly sings the staring owl,

Tu-whit;

Tu-who, a merry note,
While greasy Joan doth keel the pot.

(*Love's Labour's Lost*, Act V, scene ii)

The weird sisters, hand in hand,
Posters of the sea and land,
Thus do go, about, about,
Thrice to thine, and thrice to mine,
And thrice again, to make up nine.
Peace! the charm's wound up.

(*Macbeth*, Act I, scene iii)

Double, double, toil and trouble;
Fire burn and cauldron bubble.
Fillet of a fenny snake,
In the cauldron boil and bake;
Eye of newt and toe of frog,
Wool of bat and tongue of dog,
Adder's fork and blind-worm's sting,
Lizard's leg and howlet's wing,
For a charm of powerful trouble,
Like a hell-broth boil and bubble.
Double, double, toil and trouble;
Fire burn and cauldron bubble.
Cool it with a baboon's blood,
Then the charm is firm and good.

(*Macbeth*, Act IV, scene i)

Over hill, over dale,
　　Thorough bush, thorough brier,
Over park, over pale,
　　Thorough flood, thorough fire,
I do wander every where,
Swifter than the moon's sphere;
And I serve the fairy queen,
To dew her orbs upon the green.

(*A Midsummer Night's Dream*, Act II, scene i)

15

I know a bank where the wild thyme blows,
Where oxlips and the nodding violet grows,
Quite over-canopied with luscious woodbine,
With sweet musk-roses, and with eglantine;
There sleeps Titania some time of the night,
Lull'd in these flowers with dances and delight;
And there the snake throws her enamell'd skin,
Weed wide enough to wrap a fairy in.

(*A Midsummer Night's Dream*, Act II, scene i)

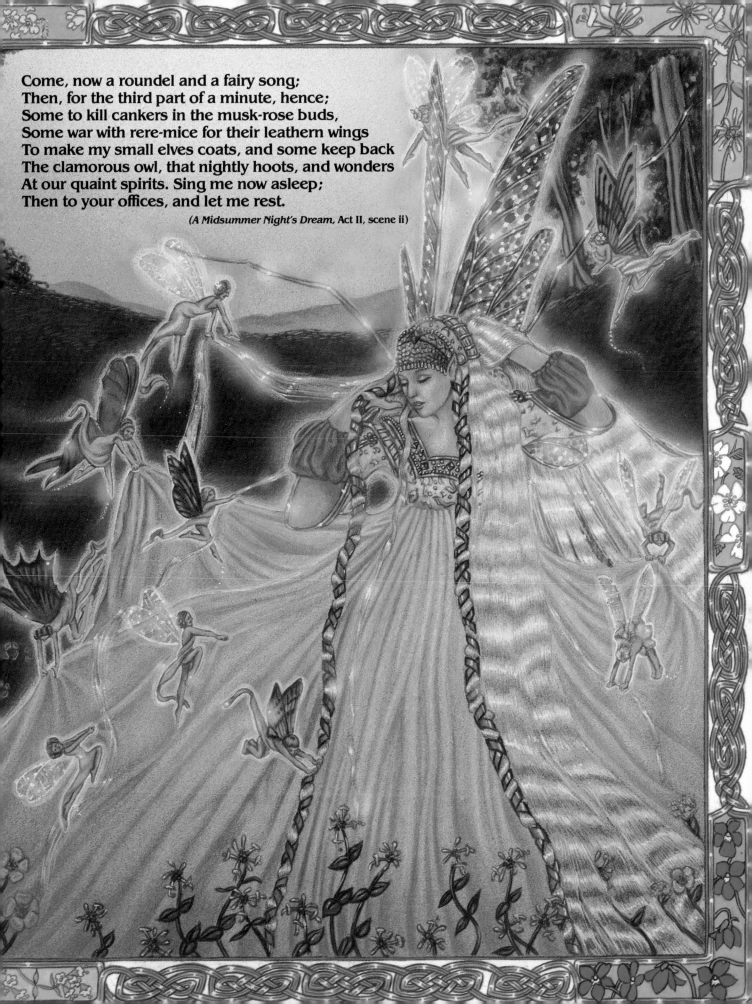

Come, now a roundel and a fairy song;
Then, for the third part of a minute, hence;
Some to kill cankers in the musk-rose buds,
Some war with rere-mice for their leathern wings
To make my small elves coats, and some keep back
The clamorous owl, that nightly hoots, and wonders
At our quaint spirits. Sing me now asleep;
Then to your offices, and let me rest.

(A Midsummer Night's Dream, Act II, scene ii)

You spotted snakes with double tongue,
   Thorny hedge-hogs, be not seen;
Newts, and blind-worms, do no wrong;
   Come not near our fairy queen.
     Philomel, with melody
     Sing in our sweet lullaby;
Lulla, lulla, lullaby; lulla, lulla, lullaby.
      Never harm
      Nor spell nor charm,
     Come our lovely lady nigh;
     So, good night, with lullaby.

Weaving spiders, come not here;
   Hence, you long-legg'd spinners, hence!
Beetles black, approach not near;
   Worm nor snail, do no offence.

     Philomel, with melody
     Sing in our sweet lullaby;
Lulla, lulla, lullaby; lulla, lulla, lullaby.
      Never harm,
      Nor spell nor charm,
     Come our lovely lady nigh;
     So, good night, with lullaby.

(A Midsummer Night's Dream, Act II, scene ii)

18

Bottom. I see their knavery. This is to make an ass of me, to fright me, if they could; but I will not stir from this place, do what they can. I will walk up and down here, and I will sing, that they shall hear I am not afraid (Sings)

> The woosel cock so black of hue,
>   With orange-tawny bill,
> The throstle with his note so true,
>   The wren with little quill—

Titania. (Awakening) What angel wakes me from my flow'ry bed?

Bottom.(Sings)

> The finch, the sparrow, and the lark,
>   The plain-song cuckoo grey,
> Whose note full many a man doth mark,
>   And dares not answer nay—

for indeed, who would set his wit to so foolish a bird?
Who would give a bird the lie, though he cry "cuckoo" never so?

Titania.   I pray thee, gentle mortal, sing again.
Mine ear is much enamor'd of thy note;
So is mine eye enthralled to thy shape;
And thy fair virtue's force doth move me
On the first views to say, to swear, I love thee.

Bottom. Methinks, mistress, you should have little reason for that. And yet, to say the truth, reason and love keep little company together now-a-days. The more the pity that some honest neighbors will not make them friends. Nay, I can gleek upon occasion.

Titania. Thou art as wise as thou art beautiful.

Bottom. Not so, neither; but if I had wit enough to get out of this wood, I have enough to serve mine own turn.

Titania. Out of this wood do not desire to go;
Thou shalt remain here, whether thou wilt or no.
I am a spirit of no common rate;
The summer still doth tend upon my state;
And I do love thee; therefore go with me.
I'll give thee fairies to attend on thee;
And they shall fetch thee jewels from the deep,
And sing while thou on pressed flowers dost sleep.
And I will purge thy mortal grossness so,
That thou shalt like an airy spirit go.
Peaseblossom! Cobweb! Moth! and Mustardseed!

1 Fairy.   Ready.

2 Fairy.   And I.

3 Fairy.   And I.

4 Fairy.   Where shall we go?

Titania . Be kind and courteous to this gentleman,
Hop in his walks and gambol in his eyes;
Feed him with apricocks and dewberries,
With purple grapes, green figs, and mulberries;
The honey–bags steal from the humble bees,
And for night–tapers crop their waxen thighs,
And light them at the fiery glow-worm's eyes,
To have my love to bed and to arise;
And pluck the wings from painted butterflies,
To fan the moonbeams from his sleeping eyes.
Nod to him, elves, and do him courtesies.

(A Midsummer Night's Dream, Act III, scene i)

Through the house give glimmering light
    By the dead and drowsy fire;
Every elf and fairy sprite
    Hop as light as bird from brier;
And this ditty after me
Sing, and dance it trippingly.

First, rehearse your song by rote,
To each word a warbling note:
Hand in hand, with fairy grace,
Will we sing, and bless this place.

(*A Midsummer Night's Dream*, Act V, sc. i)

Orpheus with his lute made trees,
And the mountain tops that freeze,
    Bow themselves when he did sing.
To his music plants and flowers
Ever sprung, as sun and showers
    There had made a lasting spring.

Every thing that heard him play,
Even the billows of the sea,
    Hung their heads and then lay by.
In sweet music is such art,
Killing care and grief of heart
    Fall asleep, or hearing, die.

(*King Henry VIII*, Act III, scene i)

Where the bee sucks, there suck I,
In a cowslip's bell I lie;
There I couch when owls do cry.
On the bat's back I do fly
After summer merrily.
Merrily, merrily shall I live now,
Under the blossom that hangs on the bough.

(*The Tempest*, Act V, scene i)

Romeo. I dream'd a dream tonight.
Mercutio. And so did I.
Romeo. Well, what was yours?
Mercutio. That dreamers often lie.
Romeo. In bed asleep, while they do dream things true
Mercutio. O! then I see Queen Mab hath been with you.
She is the fairies' midwife, and she comes
In shape no bigger than an agate-stone
On the forefinger of an alderman,
Drawn with a team of little atomies
Over men's noses as they lie asleep.
Her chariot is an empty hazel-nut,
Made by the joiner squirrel or old grub,
Time out o' mind the fairies' coach-makers.
Her waggon-spokes made of long spinners' legs;
The cover, of the wings of grasshoppers;
Her traces, of the smallest spider's web;
Her collars, of the moonshine's watery beams;
Her whip, of cricket's bone; the lash, of film;
Her waggoner, a small grey-coated gnat,
Not half so big as a round little worm
Prick'd from the lazy finger of a maid.
And in this state she gallops night by night
Through lovers' brains, and then they dream of
      love.

(Romeo and Juliet, Act I, scene iv)

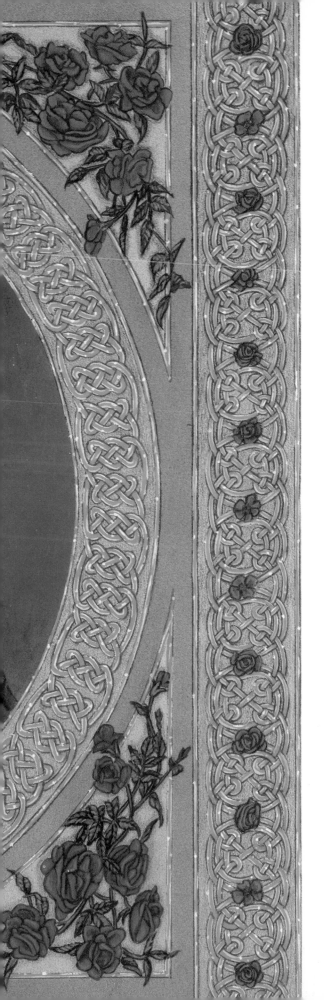

See how she leans her cheek upon her hand!
O that I were a glove upon that hand
That I might touch that cheek.

(*Romeo and Juliet,* Act II, scene i)

What's in a name? That which we call a rose
By any other name would smell as sweet.
So Romeo would, were he not Romeo call'd,
Retain that dear perfection which he owes
Without that title. Romeo, doff thy name,
And for thy name, which is no part of thee,
Take all myself.

(*Romeo and Juliet,* Act II, scene i)

Hark, hark, the lark at heaven's gate sings,
And Phoebus 'gins arise,
His steeds to water at those springs
On chaliced flowers that lies;
And winking Mary-buds begin
To ope their golden eyes;
With every thing that pretty is,
My lady sweet, arise:
Arise, arise!

32

(*Cymbeline*, Act II, scene iii)

O mistress mine, where are you
    roaming?
O, stay and hear, your true love's
    coming,
    That can sing both high and low.
Trip no further, pretty sweeting;
Journeys end in lovers meeting,
    Every wise man's son doth know.

(*Twelfth Night*, Act II, scene iii)

33

When, in disgrace with fortune and men's eyes
I all alone beweep my outcast state,
And trouble deaf heaven with my bootless cries,
And look upon myself, and curse my fate,
Wishing me like to one more rich in hope,
Featured like him, like him with friends possess'd,
Desiring this man's art, and that man's scope,
With what I most enjoy contented least;
Yet in these thoughts myself almost despising,
Haply I think on thee, and then my state,
Like to the lark at break of day arising
From sullen earth, sings hymns at heaven's gate.
    For thy sweet love remember'd such wealth brings
    That then I scorn to change my state with kings.

(Sonnet 29)

Who is Silvia? what is she,
That all our swains commend her?
Holy, fair, and wise is she;
The heaven's such grace did lend her,
    That she might admired be.

Is she kind as she is fair?
For beauty lives with kindness.
Love doth to her eyes repair,
To help him of his blindness;
    And, being help'd, inhabits there.

Then to Silvia let us sing,
That Silvia is excelling;
She excels each mortal thing.
Upon the dull earth dwelling.
    To her let us garlands bring.

(*The Two Gentlemen of Verona*, Act IV, scene ii)

It was a lover and his lass,
    With a hey, and a ho, and a hey nonino,
That o'er the green corn-field did pass,
    In spring time, the only pretty ring time,
When birds do sing, hey ding a ding, ding;
Sweet lovers love the spring.

Between the acres of the rye,
    With a hey, and a ho, and a hey nonino,
These pretty country folks would lie,
    In spring time, the only pretty ring time,
When birds do sing, hey ding a ding, ding;
Sweet lovers love the spring.

This carol they began that hour,
    With a hey, and a ho, and a hey nonino,
How that a life was but a flower
    In spring time, the only pretty ring time,
When birds do sing, hey ding a ding, ding;
    Sweet lovers love the spring.

And therefore take the present time,
    With a hey, and a ho, and a hey nonino,
For love is crowned with the prime
    In spring time, the only pretty ring time,
When birds do sing, hey ding a ding, ding;
    Sweet lovers love the spring.

(*As You Like It*, Act V, scene iii)

Shall I compare thee to a summer's day?
Thou art more lovely and more temperate:
Rough winds do shake the darling buds of May,
And summer's lease hath all too short a date:
Sometime too hot the eye of heaven shines,
And often is his gold complexion dimm'd;
And every fair from fair sometimes declines,
By chance or nature's changing course untrimm'd;
But thy eternal summer shall not fade,
Nor lose possession of that fair thou owest,
Nor shall death brag thou wander'st in his shade,
When in eternal lines to time thou growest;
    So long as men can breathe, or eyes can see,
    So long lives this, and this gives life to thee.

(Sonnet 18)

The barge she sat in, like a burnish'd throne,
Burn'd on the water. The poop was beaten gold,
Purple the sails, and so perfumed that
The winds were love-sick with them; the oars were silver,
Which to the tune of flutes kept stroke, and made
The water which they beat to follow faster,
As amorous of their strokes. For her own person,
It beggar'd all description: she did lie
In her pavilion—cloth-of-gold of tissue—
O'er-picturing that Venus where we see
The fancy outwork nature; on each side her
Stood pretty dimpled boys, like smiling Cupids,
With divers-colour'd fans, whose wind did seem
To glow the delicate cheeks which they did cool,
And what they undid did.

Her gentlewomen, like the Nereides,
So many mermaids, tended her i' the eyes,
And made their bends adornings. At the helm
A seeming mermaid steers; the silken tackle
Swell with the touches of those flower-soft hands,
That yarely frame the office. From the barge
A strange invisible perfume hits the sense
Of the adjacent wharfs. The city cast
Her people out upon her; and Antony,
Enthron'd i' the market-place, did sit alone,
Whistling to the air, which, but for vacancy,
Had gone to gaze on Cleopatra too
And made a gap in nature.

(Antony and Cleopatra, Act II, scene ii) 41

Her father lov'd me; oft invited me,
Still question'd me the story of my life
From year to year, the battles, sieges, fortunes
That I have pass'd.
I ran it through, even from my boyish days
To th' very moment that he bade me tell it.
Wherein I spake of most disastrous chances,
Of moving accidents by flood and field,
Of hair-breadth 'scapes i' th' imminent deadly breach,
Of being taken by the insolent foe
And sold to slavery, of my redemption thence
And portance in my traveller's history.
Wherein of antres vast and deserts idle,
Rough quarries, rocks and hills whose heads touch heaven,
It was my hint to speak (such was the process),
And of the Cannibals that each other eat,
The Anthropophagi, and men whose heads
Do grow beneath their shoulders. This to hear
Would Desdemona seriously incline;
But still the house-affairs would draw her thence,

Which ever as she could with haste dispatch
She'd come again, and with a greedy ear
Devour up my discourse. Which I observing,
Took once a pliant hour and found good means
To draw from her a prayer of earnest heart
That I would all my pilgrimage dilate,
Whereof by parcels she had something heard,
But not intentively. I did consent;
And often did beguile her of her tears,
When I did speak of some distressful stroke
That my youth suffer'd. My story being done,
She gave me for my pains a world of sighs.
She swore, i' faith, 'twas strange, 'twas passing strange;
'Twas pitiful, 'twas wondrous pitiful.
She wish'd she had not heard it, yet she wish'd
That heaven had made her such a man. She thank'd me,
And bade me, if I had a friend that lov'd her,
I should but teach him how to tell my story,
And that would woo her. Upon this hint I spake.
She lov'd me for the dangers I had pass'd,
And I lov'd her that she did pity them.
This only is the witchcraft I have us'd.

44   (*Othello*, Act I, scene iii)

All furnish'd, all in arms;
All plum'd like estridges, that with the wind
Bated like eagles having lately bath'd,
Glittering in golden coats like images,
As full of spirit as the month of May,
And gorgeous as the sun at midsummer;
Wanton as youthful goats, wild as young bulls.
I saw young Harry with his beaver on,
His cushes on his thighs, gallantly arm'd,
Rise from the ground like feather'd Mercury,
And vaulted with such ease into his seat
As if an angel dropp'd down from the clouds
To turn and wind a fiery Pegasus,
And witch the world with noble horsemanship.

(King Henry IV, Part One, Act IV, scene i)

This day is call'd the feast of Crispian:
He that outlives this day, and comes safe home,
Will stand a tip-toe when this day is named,
And rouse him at the name of Crispian.
He that shall live this day, and see old age,
Will yearly on the vigil feast his neighbours,
And say 'Tomorrow is Saint Crispian.'
Then will he strip his sleeve and show his scars,
And say 'These wounds I had on Crispin's day.'
Old men forget; yet all shall be forgot,
But he'll remember with advantages
What feats he did that day. Then shall our names,
Familiar in his mouth as household words,
Harry the king, Bedford and Exeter,
Warwick and Talbot, Salisbury and Gloucester,
Be in their flowing cups freshly remember'd.
This story shall the good man teach his son;
And Crispin Crispian shall ne'er go by,
From this day to the ending of the world,
But we in it shall be remembered—
We few, we happy few, we band of brothers;
For he today that sheds his blood with me
Shall be my brother; be he ne'er so vile,
This day shall gentle his condition;
And gentlemen in England now abed
Shall think themselves accurs'd they were not here;
And hold their manhoods cheap whiles any speaks
That fought with us upon Saint Crispin's day.

(*King Henry V,* Act IV, scene iii)

The master, the swabber, the boatswain, and I,
    The gunner and his mate,
Loved Mall, Meg, and Marian, and Margery,
    But none of us car'd for Kate;
    For she had a tongue with a tang,
    Would cry to a sailor, "Go hang!"
She loved not the savour of tar, nor of pitch,
Yet a tailor might scratch her where e'er she did itch.
    Then to sea, boys, and let her go hang!

(*The Tempest*, Act II, scene ii)

51

Come, thou monarch of the vine,
Plumpy Bacchus with pink eyne!
In thy vats our cares be drown'd,
With thy grapes our hairs be crown'd!
Cup us, till the world go round,
Cup us, till the world go round!

(*Antony and Cleopatra,* Act II, scene vii)

Crabbed age and youth cannot live together:
Youth is full of pleasance, age is full of care,
Youth like summer morn, age like winter weather,
Youth like summer brave, age like winter bare.
Youth is full of sport, age's breath is short,
    Youth is nimble, age is lame,
Youth is hot and bold, age is weak and cold,
    Youth is wild, and age is tame.
Age, I do abhor thee, youth, I do adore thee:
    O! my love, my love is young:
Age, I do defy thee. O! sweet shepherd, hie thee,
    For methinks thou stay'st too long.

(The Passionate Pilgrim)

When my love swears that she is made of truth,
I do believe her, though I know she lies,
That she might think me some untutor'd youth,
Unlearned in the world's false subtilties.
Thus vainly thinking that she thinks me young,
Although she knows my days are past the best,
Simply I credit her false-speaking tongue;
On both sides thus is simple truth suppress'd.
But wherefore says she not she is unjust?
And wherefore say not I that I am old?
O, love's best habit is in seeming trust,
And age in love loves not t' have years told.
    Therefore I lie with her, and she with me,
    And in our faults by lies we flattered be.

(Sonnet 138)

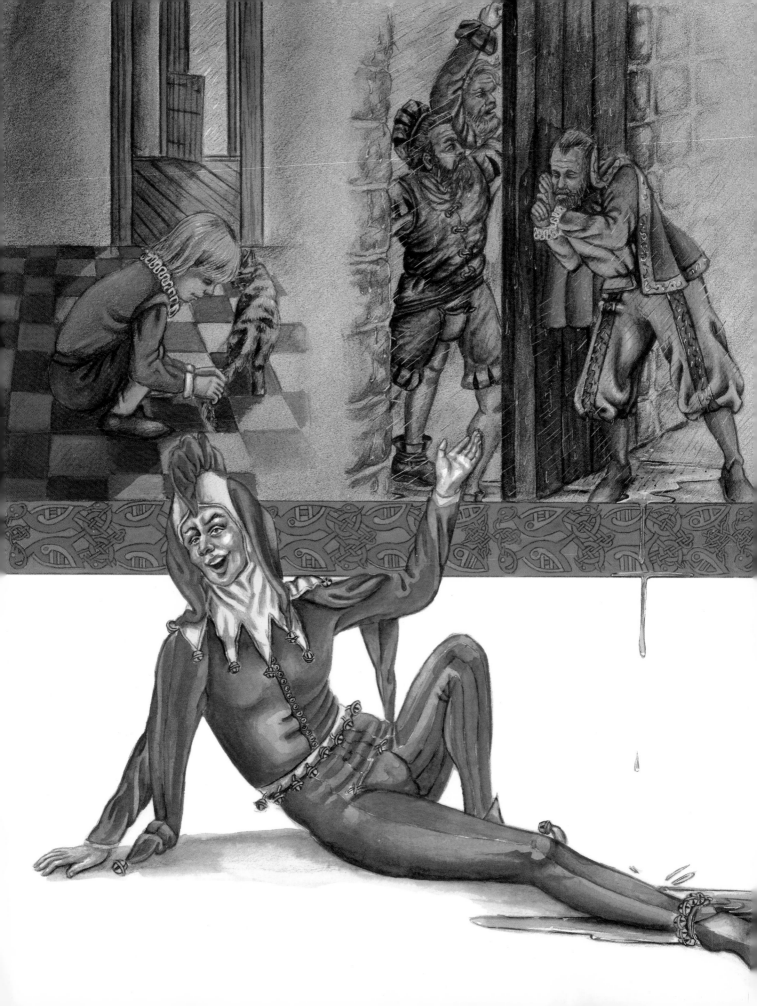

When that I was and a little tiny boy,
    With hey, ho, the wind and the rain;
A foolish thing was but a toy,
    For the rain it raineth every day.

But when I came to man's estate,
    With hey, ho, the wind and the rain;
'Gainst knaves and thieves men shut their gate,
    For the rain it raineth every day.

But when I came, alas! to wive,
    With hey, ho, the wind and the rain;
By swaggering could I never thrive,
    For the rain it raineth every day.

But when I came unto my beds,
    With hey, ho, the wind and the rain;
With toss-pots still had drunken heads,
    For the rain it raineth every day.

A great while ago the world begun,
    With hey, ho, the wind and the rain;
But that's all one, our play is done,
    And we'll strive to please you every day.

(Twelfth-Night; Or, What You Will, Act V, scene i)   57

Blow, blow, thou winter wind,
Thou art not so unkind
  As man's ingratitude;
  Thy tooth is not so keen,
  Because thou art not seen,
    Although thy breath be rude.
Heigh-ho! sing, heigh-ho! unto the green holly;
Most friendship is feigning, most loving mere folly.
    Then heigh-ho, the holly!
    This life is most jolly.

Freeze, freeze, thou bitter sky,
That does not bite so nigh
  As benefits forgot:
  Though thou the waters warp,
  Thy sting is not so sharp
    As friend remember'd not.
Heigh-ho! sing, heigh-ho! unto the green holly:
Most friendship is feigning, most loving mere folly.
    Then heigh-ho, the holly!
    This life is most jolly.

(*As You Like It,* Act II, scene vii)

59

To be, or not to be, that is the question:
Whether 'tis nobler in the mind to suffer
The slings and arrows of outrageous fortune,
Or to take arms against a sea of troubles,
And by opposing, end them. To die, to sleep—
No more, and by a sleep to say we end
The heart-ache and the thousand natural shocks
That flesh is heir to; 'tis a consummation
Devoutly to be wish'd. To die, to sleep—
To sleep, perchance to dream— ay, there's the rub,
For in that sleep of death what dreams may come,
When we have shuffled off this mortal coil,
Must give us pause; there's the respect
That makes calamity of so long life:
For who would bear the whips and scorns of time,
Th' oppressor's wrong, the proud man's contumely,
The pangs of despis'd love, the law's delay,
The insolence of office, and the spurns
That patient merit of th' unworthy takes,
When he himself might his quietus make
With a bare bodkin; who would fardels bear,
To grunt and sweat under a weary life,
But that the dread of something after death,
The undiscover'd country, from whose bourn
No traveller returns, puzzles the will,
And makes us rather bear those ills we have,
Than fly to others that we know not of?
Thus conscience does make cowards of us all,
And thus the native hue of resolution
Is sicklied o'er with the pale cast of thought,
And enterprises of great pitch and moment
With this regard their currents turn awry,
And lose the name of action.

(*Hamlet*, Act III, scene i)

60

There is a willow grows aslant the brook,
That shows his hoary leaves in the glassy stream;
Therewith fantastic garlands did she make
Of crow-flowers, nettles, daisies, and long purples
That liberal shepherds give a grosser name,
But our cold maids do dead men's fingers call them.
There, on the pendant boughs her coronet weeds
Clambering to hang, an envious sliver broke,
When down her weedy trophies and herself
Fell in the weeping brook. Her clothes spread wide,
And, mermaid-like awhile they bore her up;
Which time she chanted snatches of old tunes,
As one incapable of her own distress,
Or like a creature native and indued
Unto that element. But long it could not be
Till that her garments, heavy with their drink,
Pull'd the poor wretch from her melodious lay
To muddy death.

(*Hamlet*, Act IV, scene vii)   63

My mother had a maid call'd Barbara;
She was in love, and he she loved proved mad
And did forsake her; she had a song of 'willow';
An old thing 't was, but it express'd her fortune,
And she died singing it; that song tonight
Will not go from my mind; I have much to do
But to go hang my head all at one side,
And sing it like poor Barbara.

(*Othello*, Act IV, scene iii)

Tomorrow, and tomorrow, and tomorrow,
Creeps in this petty pace from day to day,
To the last syllable of recorded time;
And all our yesterdays have lighted fools
The way to dusty death. Out, out, brief candle!
Life's but a walking shadow, a poor player,
That struts and frets his hour upon the stage,
And then is heard no more. It is a tale
Told by an idiot, full of sound and fury,
signifying nothing.

(*Macbeth*, Act V, scene v)

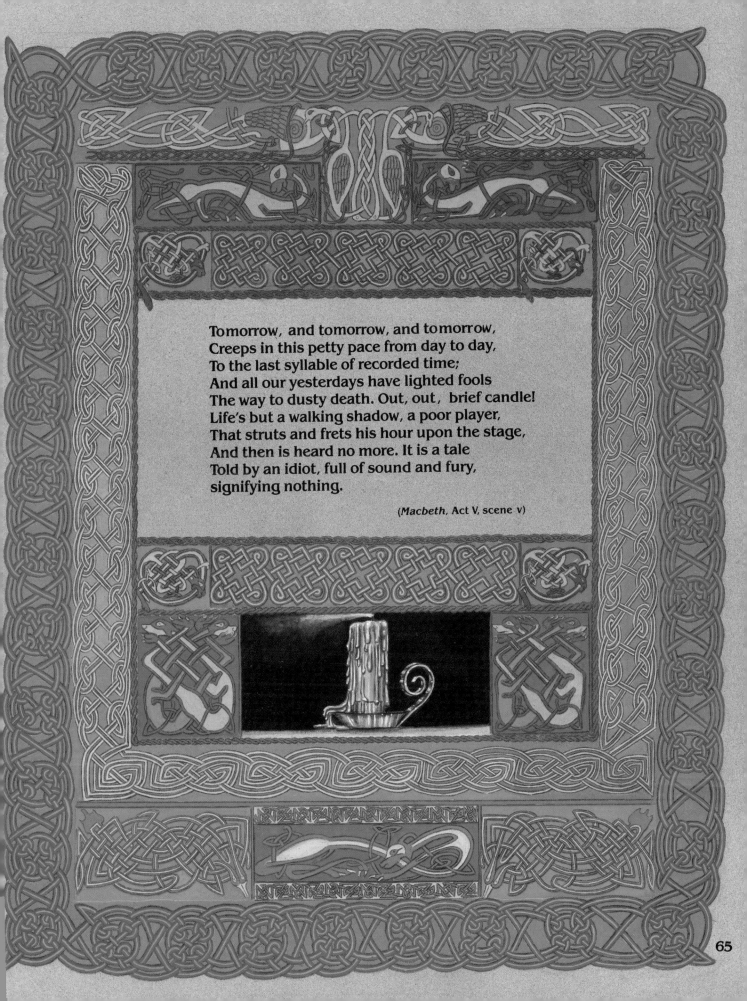

Fear no more the heat o' the sun,
　　Nor the furious winter's rages,
Thou thy worldly task hast done,
　　Home art gone, and ta'en thy wages.
Golden lads and girls all must,
As chimney-sweepers, come to dust.

Fear no more the frown o' the great,
　　Thou art past the tyrant's stroke;
Care no more to clothe and eat,
　　To thee the reed is as the oak.
The sceptre, learning, physic, must
All follow this, and come to dust.

Fear no more the lightning-flash.
　　Nor the all-dreaded thunder-stone.
Fear not slander, censure rash.
　　Thou hast finish'd joy and moan.
All lovers young, all lovers must
Consign to thee and come to dust.

No exorciser harm thee.
Nor no witchcraft charm thee.
Ghost unlaid forbear thee.
Nothing ill come near thee.
Quiet consummation have,
And renowned be thy grave.

(*Cymbeline*, Act IV, scene ii)

Full fathom five thy father lies;
    Of his bones are coral made,
Those are pearls that were his eyes,
    Nothing of him that doth fade,
But doth suffer a sea-change
Into something rich and strange.
Sea-nymphs hourly ring his knell:
            Ding-dong.
Hark! now I hear them, — Ding-dong bell.

(*The Tempest*, Act I, scene ii)

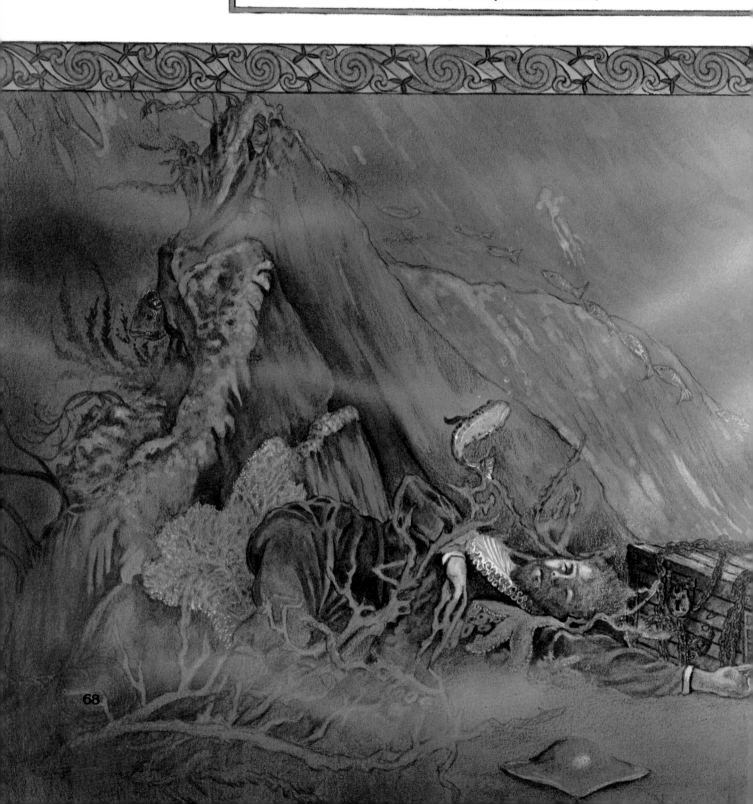

All the world's a stage,
And all the men and women merely players:
They have their exits and their entrances,
And one man in his time plays many parts,
His acts being seven ages. At first the infant,
Mewling and puking in the nurse's arms.
Then the whining school-boy, with his satchel

And shining morning face, creeping like snail
Unwillingly to school. And then the lover,
Sighing like furnace, with a woeful ballad
Made to his mistress' eyebrow. Then a soldier,
Full of strange oaths, and bearded like the pard,
Jealous in honour, sudden, and quick in quarrel,
Seeking the bubble reputation

Even in the cannon's mouth, And then the justice,
In fair round belly with good capon lined,
With eyes severe and beard of formal cut,
Full of wise saws and modern instances;
And so he plays his part. The sixth age shifts
Into the lean and slipper'd pantaloon,
With spectacles on nose and pouch on side,

His youthful hose well saved, a world too wide
For his shrunk shank, and his big manly voice,
Turning again toward childish treble, pipes
And whistles in his sound. Last scene of all,
That ends this strange eventful history,
Is second childishness, and mere oblivion,
Sans teeth, sans eyes, sans taste, sans every thing.

(*As You Like It*, Act II, scene vii)

If we shadows have offended,
Think but this, and all is mended,
That you have but slumber'd here
While these visions did appear.
And this weak and idle theme,
No more yielding but a dream,
Gentles, do not reprehend.
If you pardon, we will mend.
And, as I am an honest Puck,
If we have unearned luck
Now to scape the serpent's tongue,
We will make amends ere long;
Else the Puck a liar call.
So, good night unto you all.
Give me your hands, if we be friends,
And Robin shall restore amends.

(*A Midsummer Night's Dream*, Act V, scene i)

74

GLOSSARY

Note: Acts and scenes are here indicated in Arabic numerals; the more traditional Roman numerals are cited under the selections themselves.

Advantages	Embellishments; with exaggeration. See *King Henry V,* Act 4, scene 3 (p. 48).
Alderman	A governing official. See *Romeo and Juliet,* Act 1, scene 4 (p. 28).
Anthropophagi	Cannibals. See *Othello,* Act 1, scene 3 (p. 43).
Antres	Caves. See *Othello,* Act I, scene 3 (p. 43).
Atomies	Tiny creatures. See *Romeo and Juliet,* Act 1, scene 4 (p. 28).
Awry	Askew; twisted; on the wrong course or path. See *Hamlet,* Act 3, scene 1 (p. 62).
Bacchus	The Roman god of wine identified with the Greek Dionysus. The son of Jupiter and Semele, Bacchus was renowned for his drinking and frolicking, as invoked in *Antony and Cleopatra,* Act 2, scene 7 (p. 54).
Bated	A falconry term referring to the beating of birds' wings. In *King Henry IV, Part One,* Act 4, scene 1 (p. 47), the word can be read as "beat their wings."
Beaver	Helmet. See *King Henry IV, Part One,* Act 4, scene 1 (p. 47).
Benefits	Advantages; acts of charity; helpfulness. See *As You Like It,* Act 2, scene 7 (p. 59).
Blind-worms	Small lizards. See *Macbeth,* Act 4, scene 1 (p. 13). See also *A Midsummer Night's Dream,* Act 2, scene 2 (p. 18).
"Blows his nails"	"Blows on his nails." See *Love's Labour's Lost,* Act 5, scene 2 (p. 10).
Boatswain	An officer in charge of a ship's deck crew. See *The Tempest,* Act 2, scene 2 (p. 51).
Bodkin	A dagger. See *Hamlet,* Act 3, scene 1 (p. 60).
Bootless	Useless; unavailable. See *Sonnet 29,* (p. 34).
Bourn	Boundary. See *Hamlet,* Act 3, scene 1 (p. 60).
Brooding	Sulking, or in *Love's Labour's Lost,* Act 5, scene 2 (p. 11), perhaps the poet means warming their young or hatching eggs.
Burnished	Smooth; polished. See *Antony and Cleopatra,* Act 2, scene 2 (p. 41).
Cankers	Cankerworms: striped, green caterpillars that eat tree leaves. See *A Midsummer Night's Dream,* Act 2, scene 2 (p. 17).
Capon	A rooster that has been castrated to make it fatter for eating. In *As You Like It,* Act 2, scene 7 (p. 72), "capon lin'd" is, perhaps, a reference to the bribing of judges with capons.
Chaliced	Cup-like. See *Cymbeline,* Act 2, scene 3 (p. 32).
Collars	The cushioned parts of a harness that push against the shoulders of a draft animal. See *Romeo and Juliet,* Act 1, scene 4 (p. 28).
"Come to dust"	Die; a reference to the decay of bodies into dust. See *Cymbeline,* Act 4, scene 2 (p. 66).
Consign	To deliver, despatch or submit. See *Cymbeline,* Act 4, scene 2 (p. 66).
Consummation	Completion; ending; fulfillment. See *Hamlet,* Act 3, scene 1 (p. 60). See also *Cymbeline,* Act 4, scene 2 (p. 66).
Contumely	Rudeness; contemptuous attitude. See *Hamlet,* Act 3, scene 1 (p. 60).
Coronet	Small crown. In the context of *Hamlet,* Act 4, scene 7 (p. 63), the term is used as an adjective meaning crown-like, or similar to a coronet.
Cowslip	A flowering plant. See *The Tempest,* Act 5, scene 1 (p. 26).
Crabbed	Complicated; irritable and perverse. In "The Passionate Pilgrim," (p. 54) either or both meanings of the term can be inferred.

Crispian	An early Christian martyr, patron saint of the shoemakers. The feast of Crispian, also called St. Crispin's Day, referred to in *King Henry V*, Act 4, scene 3 (p. 48), occurred each 25th of October.
Cupids	Cupid was the Roman god of love, often identified with the Greek god Eros, and the son of Venus, goddess of love and beauty. In *Antony and Cleopatra*, Act 2, scene 2 (p. 41), the "cupids" reference is to the depiction of Cupid as a small winged boy in much classical art.
"Cup us"	"Drink to us" or "Drink to our health." See *Antony and Cleopatra*, Act 2, scene 7 (p. 52).
Cushes	Plate armor for the thighs. See *King Henry IV, Part One*, Act 4, scene 1 (p. 48).
Dilate	To relate at length, expand upon, In *Othello*, Act 1, scene 3 (p. 44).
Divers	Various; several. In *Antony and Cleopatra*, Act 2, scene 2 (p. 41), "divers-colour'd" can be read as "many-coloured."
Doff	To discard; to remove. See *Romeo and Juliet*, Act 2, scene 2 (p. 31).
Eglantine	Sweetbrier, a variety of rose. See *A Midsummer Night's Dream*, Act 2, scene 1 (p. 16).
Estridges	Ostriches. See *King Henry IV, Part One*, Act 4, scene 1 (p. 47).
Exorciser	Conjurer; a raiser of spirits. See *Cymbeline*, Act 4, scene 2 (p. 66).
Fardels	Burdens. See *Hamlet*, Act 3, scene 1 (p. 60).
Fillet	Slice. See *Macbeth*, Act 1, scene 3 (p. 13).
Frame	Perform. As in "yarely frame," *Antony and Cleopatra*, Act 2, scene 2 (p. 41). See definition for "yarely."
Furnished	Equipped. See *King Henry IV, Part One*, Act 4, scene 1 (p. 47).
Gambol	Frolic; play. See *A Midsummer Night's Dream*, Act 3, scene 1 (p. 20).
Gentle his condition	"To make him a gentleman," or "to raise his rank." See *Henry V*, Act 4, scene 3 (p. 48).
'Gins	A contraction for 'begins to.' See *Cymbeline*, Act 2, scene 3 (p. 32).
Gleek	Jest; make fun of; gibe. See *Midsummer Night's Dream*, Act 3, scene 1 (p. 20).
Grub	The worm-like larva of certain insects and beetles. See *Romeo and Juliet*, Act 1, scene 4 (p. 28).
Gunner	The cannon operator on a sailing ship. See *The Tempest*, Act 2, scene 2 (p. 51).
Hence	In *A Midsummer Night's Dream*, Act 2, scene 2 (p. 17), a command, "Get away."
Hie	Hasten; quicken. See "The Passionate Pilgrim" (p. 54).
Hoary	Gray-white; old or ancient. In *Hamlet*, (p. 63) either meaning can be taken.
Howlet	Owlet or baby owl. See *Macbeth*, Act 4, scene 1 (p. 13).
Incline	To lean or slant; to be disposed towards something. In *Othello*, Act 1, scene 3 (p. 43), the latter is meant.
Indued	Habituated; having the qualities of. See *Hamlet*, Act 4, scene 7 (p. 63).
Intentively	With attention. See *Othello*, Act 1, scene 3 (p. 44).
Joiner	Cabinet-maker. See *Romeo and Juliet*, Act 1, scene 4 (p. 28).
Keel	Stir. *Love's Labour's Lost*, Act 5, scene 2 (p. 10).
Knell	The sound of a bell; a mournful sound; an omen of sorrow or death. In *The Tempest*, Act 1, scene 2 (p. 68), any of these three meanings may be applicable.
Lay	A ballad or song. From the Old French "lai." See *Hamlet*, Act 4, scene 7 (p. 63).
Lease	Allotted time. See *Sonnet 18* (p. 38).
Liberal	In *Hamlet*, Act 4, scene 7 (p. 63), the word means free-spoken.
"Long purples"	Wild orchids. See *Hamlet*, Act 4, scene 7 (p. 63).
Mary-buds	Marigolds. See *Cymbeline*, Act 2, scene 3 (p. 32).
Mercury	In Roman mythology, the messenger of the gods, identified with the Greek Hermes.

"Winged Mercury" in *Henry IV, Part One*, Act 2, scene 7 (p. 47) refers to the winged sandals which gave Mercury the power of flight.

Mewling	Crying. See *As You Like It*, Act 2, scene 7 (p. 70).
"Mortal coil"	In *Hamlet*, Act 3, scene 1 (p. 60), the phrase means the turmoil of mortal life.
"Native hue"	In *Hamlet*, Act 3, scene 1 (p. 60), natural or healthy complexion.
Nereides	Sea nymphs, daughters of Nereus. See *Antony and Cleopatra*, Act 2, scene 2 (p. 41).
Nigh	Near; mean and stingy. Most often used in the latter sense, as in *A Midsummer Night's Dream*, Act 2, scene 2 (p. 18); but in *As You Like It*, Act 2, scene 7 (p. 57) either meaning is possible.
"O'er-picturing ...nature"	In *Antony and Cleopatra*, Act 2, scene 2 (p. 41), refers to Apelles' picture of Venus, in which the painter's art was said to be greater than nature.
Offices	Duties. See *A Midsummer Night's Dream*, Act 2, scene 2 (p. 17).
Ope	Open. See *Cymbeline*, Act 2, scene 3 (p. 32).
Orbs	Circles or balls, usually referring to the orbits of planets or to planets themselves. In *A Midsummer Night's Dream*, Act 2, scene 1 (p. 15), "orbs" can be read as "fairy rings."
Orpheus	In Greek mythology, Orpheus was the son of Calliope, the muse of heroic poetry. As a musician, Orpheus' skill was so great that nature itself stopped to listen. See *King Henry VIII*, Act 3, scene 1 (p. 25).
Oxslips	Yellow-flowered wild primulas. See *A Midsummer Night's Dream*, Act 2, scene 1 (p. 16).
Pale	Enclosure. See *A Midsummer Night's Dream*, Act 2, scene 1 (p. 15).
"Pale cast"	Pallor. See *Hamlet*, Act 3, scene 1 (p. 60).
Pantaloon	A foolish old man, from the name of a stock character in the Commedia del Arte. See *As You Like It*, Act 2, scene 7 (p. 72).
Pard	Leopard or some other large cat. See *As You Like it*, Act 2, scene 7 (p. 71).
Passing	Of brief duration; transitory. In *Othello*, Act 2, scene 3 (p. 44), the term means surpassing or very.
Pegasus	A mythological winged horse that was born out of the blood of the slain, snake-haired Medusa. See *King Henry IV, Part One*, Act 4, scene 1 (p. 47).
Pendant	Hanging; something suspended from above. See *Hamlet*, Act 4, scene 7 (p. 63).
Philomel	A nightingale. In Ovid's *Metamorphosis*, Philomela, the daughter of King Pandion of Athens, was turned into a nightingale. See *A Midsummer Night's Dream*, Act 2, scene 2 (p. 18).
Phoebus	A Roman name for the Greek god of the sun, Apollo. See *Cymbeline*, Act 2, scene 3 (p. 32).
Physic	Medical science. See *Cymbeline*, Act 4, scene 2 (p. 66).
"Pink eyne"	With half-shut eyes. See *Antony and Cleopatra*, Act 2, scene 7 (p. 52).
Pitch	Height; A term from falconry, meaning the highest point in a hawk's flight. See *Hamlet*, Act 3, scene 1 (p. 60).
Plain-song	A simple melody without elaborations. See *A Midsummer Night's Dream*, Act 3, scene 1 (p. 20).
Pleasance	Gaiety. See "The Passionate Pilgrim" (p. 54).
Pliant	Convenient; favorable. See *Othello*, Act 1, scene 3 (p. 44).
Portance	Behavior. See *Othello*, Act 1, scene 3 (p. 43).
Posters	People who ride posthaste or quickly. See *Macbeth*, Act 1, scene 3 (p. 13).
Puzzles	Frustrates. See *Hamlet*, Act 3, scene 1 (p. 60).
Queen Mab	Probably an invention of Shakespeare's in *Romeo and Juliet*, Act 1, scene 5 (p. 28). The term "Mab" was common slang for slut, or woman of low repute.
Quietus	A final discharge of a duty or debt; the release from life; death. See *Hamlet*, Act 3, scene 1 (p. 60).
Repair	To go or to journey. See *The Two Gentlemen of Verona*, Act 4, scene 2 (p. 35).

Reprehend	Reprove; censure; criticize. See *A Midsummer Night's Dream*, Act 5, scene 1 (p. 74).
Rere-Mice	Bats. See *A Midsummer Night's Dream*, Act 2, scene 2 (17).
Respect	Consideration. See *Hamlet*, Act 3, scene 1 (p. 60).
Rote	A memorizing process using repetition and routine. Also a medieval stringed instrument. In *A Midsummer Night's Dream*, Act 5, scene 1 (p. 23), some pun is probably intended on the two meanings.
Roundel	A dance in a circle. See *A Midsummer Night's Dream*, Act 2, scene 2 (p. 17).
Rub	Obstacle; problem. See *Hamlet*, Act 3, scene 1 (p. 60).
Sans	Latin for "without." See *As You Like It*, Act 2, scene 7 (p. 73).
Saws	Maxims; saying. See *As You Like It*, Act 2, scene 7 (p. 72).
Scape	A variant of the word "escape." See *A Midsummer Night's Dream*, Act 5, scene 1 (p. 74).
Sceptre	Literally a rod held by royal persons, here royalty itself or power. See *Cymbeline*, Act 4, scene 2 (p. 66).
"Shuffled off"	Sloughed off; removed. See *Hamlet*, Act 3, scene 1 (p. 60).
Sicklied	Rendered sickly; with the appearance of sickness. See *Hamlet*, Act 3, scene 1 (p. 60).
Sphere	In the Ptolemaic system of astronomy, a sphere is the shape of the orbit of the moon or the planets around the earth. See *A Midsummer Night's Dream*, Act 2, scene 1 (p. 15).
Sport	Mockery; jest. See "The Passionate Pilgrim" (p. 54).
State	Mental or emotional mood; position in the world. See *Sonnet 29* (p. 34) for both meanings of the word. Line 10 has the former, line 14 the latter meaning.
Sullen	Dull; somber. See *Sonnet 29* (p. 34).
Swabber	Slang for the member of a ship's crew who mops, or "swabs" the deck. See *The Tempest*, Act 2, scene 2 (p. 51).
Throstle	A song thrush, a small bird. See *A Midsummer Night's Dream*, Act 3, scene 1 (p. 20).
Toss-pots	Drunkards. See *Twelfth Night*, Act 5, scene 1 (p. 57).
Traces	A path or a course; also the side straps or chains connecting a harnessed animal to the vehicle that it is pulling. In *Romeo and Juliet*, Act 1, scene 4 (p. 28), a pun on the two meanings is probably intended.
Trip	To go from one place to another; to stumble or fall; also to walk with a light, nimble tread. In *Twelfth Night*, Act 2, scene 3 (p. 33), all three meanings are possible and probable.
Untrimmed	Divested of beauty. See *Sonnet 18* (p. 38).
"Unto my beds"	In the context of *Twelfth Night*, Act 5, scene 1 (p. 57), the phrase probably means "old age."
Vacancy	A Reference to the vacuum caused by misplaced air. See *Antony and Cleopatra*, Act 2, scene 2 (p. 41).
Venus	The Roman goddess of love and beauty identified with the Greek Aphrodite. Mythology says that she was not born, but sprang from the sea. See *Antony and Cleopatra*, Act 2, scene 2 (p. 41).
Wanton	Immoral; cruel; frolicsome. In *King Henry IV, Part One* (p. 47), Shakespeare probably used the word in the latter sense.
Warp	Freeze. See *As You Like It*, Act 2, scene 7 (p. 59).
Weed	Clothing; a garment. See *A Midsummer Night's Dream*, Act 2, scene 2 (p. 18).
Woodbine	Honeysuckle. See *A Midsummer Night's Dream*, Act 2, scene 1 (p. 16).
Wooselcock	A male blackbird. See *A Midsummer Night's Dream*, Act 3, scene 1 (p. 20).
"Worm prick'd from the lazy finger of a maid"	Refers to an old wives' tale that worms sprang from the fingers of idle girls. See *Romeo and Juliet*, Act 1, scene 4 (p. 28).
"Wound up"	Complete and ready to be effective. See *Macbeth*, Act 1, scene 3 (p. 13).
"Yarely frame"	Deftly perform. See *Antony and Cleopatra*, Act 2, scene 2 (p. 41).

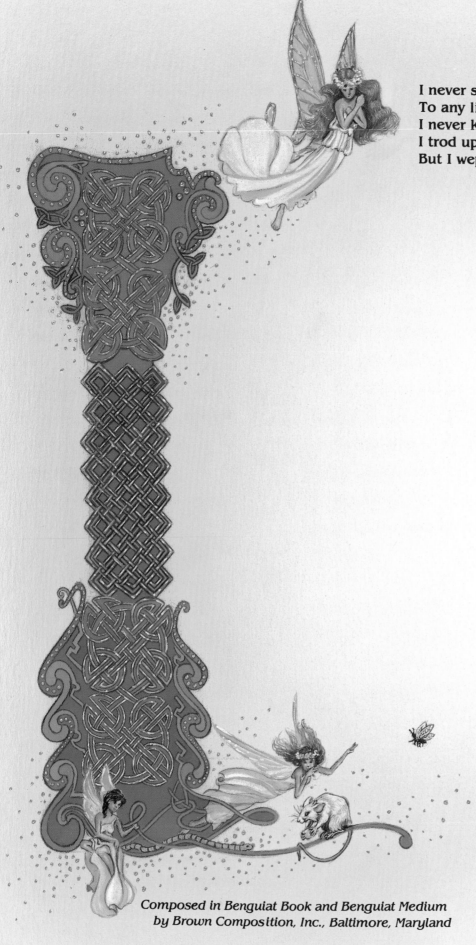

I never spake bad word, nor did ill turn
To any living creature; believe me, la,
I never kill'd a mouse, nor hurt a fly;
I trod upon a worm against my will,
But I wept for it.

(*Pericles*, Act IV, scene i)

Designed by Barbara Holdridge

*Composed in Benguiat Book and Benguiat Medium
by Brown Composition, Inc., Baltimore, Maryland*

*Printed and bound by Everbest Printing Company, Hong Kong/
Four Colour Imports, Ltd., Louisville, Kentucky*

95-50